# The Golden Rule
## Collected Wisdom

Compiled and Illustrated by Carmel Mawle

Ardea Herodias Books

*For Danny, Eliana, Liam, Ryder, and Cory.
With love, from Amma.*

The Golden Rule: Collected Wisdom. Copyright © 2025 by Carmel Mawle. All rights reserved. Printed in the United States of America. No part of this book may be used or reproduced in any manner whatsoever without written permission except in the case of brief quotations embedded in critical articles and reviews. For information, address Ardea Herodias Books, 107 Yatasi Court, Red Feather Lakes, Colorado, 80545.

First Edition
Complied and illustrated by
Carmel Mawle

Ardea Herodias Books

# Foreward

"Our life depends on the life of Mother Earth. If Mother Earth gets sick, so shall we. So, we must keep Mother Earth, including all her people, healthy – the creatures who crawl, the ones who swim, the ones who fly. The trees, the bushes, the waters, the air, and the rocks, all of these are part of Mother Earth. If we do anything to harm the balance that has been created for us – if we do anything that shows disrespect – then we are going to become sick, too."

~Frances Sanderson, Ojibway Tribe

Scientists believe our human ability to empathize with each other and work together has contributed to the survival of our species. Perhaps we have evolved with this sense of empathy and reciprocity through cultivating the earth and harvesting what nurtures us. Our collective wisdom may be rooted in the recognition that our life, our sustenance, everything we are and have comes from the earth.

In our Collected Wisdom Series, Ardea Herodias Books explores this wisdom through many traditions, faiths, and cultures. We'd like to think our children will learn the innate value of every human being in school, but parents will always be their most important teachers.

This first book explores what may be a foundational principle of civilization: empathy. "Do unto others as you would have them do unto you" is, within the Christian faith, known as "The Golden Rule." How has this principle taken shape within other faiths and cultures? I've included, here, a small sampling. I invite families to read and discuss these interpretations together. Consider how these wisdoms may have evolved. Are there subtle differences? Can we gain a new perspective by exploring these codes of conduct through a new lens? Are there examples in our daily lives that illustrate these principles?

We hope these pages, and the forthcoming Collected Wisdom Series, will inspire a love, respect, and appreciation of the earth and our fellow inhabitants.

"Our life depends on the life of Mother Earth. If Mother Earth gets sick, so shall we."

~Frances Sanderson, Ojibway Tribe

"Respect for all life is the foundation."
~Iroquois Tribe

"All things are our relatives: what we do to everything, we do to ourselves. All is really One."
~Black Elk, Lakota Tribe Elder

"Do unto others as you would have them do unto you."
~Christian Faith

"If it harms no one, do what you will."
~Paganism Faith

"What is hateful to you, do not do to your fellow man."
~Judaism Faith

"Regard your neighbor's gain as your gain, and your neighbor's loss as your loss."
~Taoism Faith

"Treat others as you'd want to be treated in their situation."
~Humanism Philosophy

"Be tolerant of those who are lost on the path."
~Black Elk, Oglala Lakota Tribe

"That nature only is good when it shall not do unto another whatever is not good for its own self."

~Zoroastrianism Faith

"I am a stranger to no one, and no one is a stranger to me. Indeed, I am a friend to all."
~Sikhism Faith

"No one among you is a believer unless he desires for his brother that which he desires for himself."
~Islam Faith

"We are all part of the universal creative force and therefore one family in God."

~Spiritualism Faith

"Just as a mother would protect her only child with her life, even so let one cultivate a boundless love for all beings."

~Buddhism Faith

A note to my young friends:

I grew up in the wilderness of Alaska. I learned to practice kindness to the animals near my home by giving them lots of room to feel safe. In real life, I would never ask a wild moose for a ride!

This is a story of a kindness that spreads through a wintry night. Can you imagine ways that you might help kindness spread among your friends and family? How can you show kindness to the earth that we share?

Kindly,

Carmel Mawle

www.ingramcontent.com/pod-product-compliance
Lightning Source LLC
Chambersburg PA
CBHW041501220426
43661CB00016B/1217